KILLER COCKTAILS

MURDEROUSLY DELICIOUS LIBATIONS
INSPIRED BY HISTORY'S
MOST NOTORIOUS KILLERS

THE CONTROVERSIAL COCKTAIL CLUB
VOLUME 2

THORA POE PIERCE &
THORNE PHOBOS PAYNE

Copyright © 2024 TPP LLP
All rights reserved.

No part of this book can be reproduced in any form or by written, electronic or mechanical, including photocopying, recording, or by any information retrieval system without written permission in writing by the author.

Printed in Great Britain

Although every precaution has been taken in the preparation of this book, the publisher and author assume no responsibility for errors or omissions. Neither is any liability assumed for damages resulting from the use of information contained herein.

ISBN 9798323291946

about us

Be introduced to the two wild and wonderful connoisseurs who are taking the world by storm.

They love a good tipple, a catchy tune, and a tall tale - but they're not too snooty about it. Along with their discerning taste, they're not afraid to get a little rowdy. In fact, they relish the seedier side of life, just for the fun of it. And let's not forget their feline muse, the one and only Gen. Pussy Talemonger - what a name, what a cat!

Together, they have embarked on a creative journey to write a series of books that are completely random, yet linked by their irreverent humour and general disregard for propriety. They don't care about respectability or purpose - they just want to make you laugh.

They've got opinions, they've got humour, and they've got a disregard for the opinions of others - especially their friends. So don't take them too seriously, and don't take yourself too seriously either...just buckle up for a wild ride.

Come and join them on this journey of whimsy and wonder, where the joy of life is celebrated with every page.

The Controversial Cocktail Club

Welcome, dear reader, to a series of cocktail books like no other – a concoction of murderously delicious libations inspired by history's most notorious killers, both real and imagined. But before you dive into this macabre mixology, be warned: this tome is steeped in tongue-in-cheek humour and not to be taken too seriously. After all, we're here to explore the dark side of history and literature with a cocktail shaker in hand, not a dagger!

So, as you turn these pages, remember: all visuals are purely for illustration purposes. We're stirring up history with a swizzle stick, not a scalpel. Don't expect a true crime exposé or a somber historical tome. Instead, prepare for a whimsical whirlwind tour through a landscape where cocktails are named after infamous characters, and the only thing we're killing is time.

Buckle up for a wild ride through a world where whimsy reigns supreme, and the joy of living is toasted with every sip. Whether you're here for the tales or the cocktails, you're in for a treat. Let the revelry begin, and remember: it's all in good spirits.

Gin

Criminal Mastermind	10
Victorian Underbelly	12
The Demon Barber	14
Witch's Brew	16
Nautilus Depth	18
Thames Mystery	20
Stern Discipline	22
Guilty Rose	24

Vodka

St. Petersburg Summer	28
Femme Fatale	30
Vampire's Rose	32
Despair on the Rocks	34
Monstrous Creation	36
Transylvanian Nightshade	38
Off with Their Heads	40
Mystic Elixir	42

Bourbon, Whisky, Whiskey

Scottish Iron	46
Secret Chamber	48
Moorland Storm	50
Marshland Escape	52
Plantation Fury	54
House of Usher	56
Wonderland Wrath	58
Thief's Reward	60
Dual Nature	62

Wine, Vermouth, Sherry

Transylvanian Night	66
Social Ascent	68
Eastern Enigma	70

Rum

High Seas Adventure	74
Monte Cristo's Revenge	76
Invisible Elixir	78
Island Experiment	80
Sailor's Delight	82
Usurper's Draught	84
Pirate's Demise	86
Catacomb Elixir	88
Ocean's Obsession	90

Tequila & Liqueur

Venetian Deceit	94
Royal Revenge	96

Brandy & Cognac

Revolutionary Spirit	100
Victorian Seduction	102
Parisian Underworld	104
Renaissance Ambition	106
Bell Tower Solitude	108
Regal Poison	110
Opera's Shadow	112
Tempter's Toast	114
Unrelenting Justice	116

Other

Sinister Sophistication	120

Behind the façade of respectable London,
Professor Moriarty's criminal empire exuded the sharp,
intellectual scent of tobacco and ink, as precise and calculating
as the mind of the 'Napoleon of Crime' himself.

Criminal Mastermind

Ingredients

2 oz London Dry Gin
1 oz Sweet Vermouth
0.5 oz Lapsang Souchong tea syrup
Lemon twist

Recipe

Infuse simple syrup with Lapsang Souchong tea.
Mix gin, vermouth, and tea syrup in a shaker with ice.
Strain into a chilled glass and garnish with a lemon twist.

Match wits with the Napoleon of Crime in a cocktail as sharp and complex as Moriarty's criminal intellect.

Bill Sikes walked the dark, grimy streets of Victorian London, his heavy boots stirring the smells of smoke and dirt, an air as menacing and ruthless as his own hardened heart.

Victorian Underbelly

Ingredients

2 oz London Dry Gin
1 oz Earl Grey tea syrup
0.5 oz Lemon juice
Dash of smoky whisky

Recipe

Brew Earl Grey tea, cool it, and make a syrup.
Shake gin, tea syrup, and lemon juice with ice.
Strain into a glass and float a dash of smoky whisky on top.

Plunge into the grimy underworld of
Dickensian London with a cocktail
that's as rough and ruthless as Bill Sikes.

In the shadowy corners of Fleet Street, Sweeney Todd's barber shop held a macabre secret, the air tainted with the scent of shaving cream and an unsettling hint of blood, as sharp and chilling as his razor.

The Demon Barber

Ingredients

2 oz Gin
1 oz Pomegranate juice
0.5 oz Lemon juice
Dash of cream

Recipe

Shake gin, pomegranate juice, and lemon juice with ice.
Strain into a glass and carefully layer a dash of cream on top.

Indulge in a macabre mix that's as intriguing and sinister as Sweeney Todd's infamous barber shop.

Medea, cloaked in her knowledge of sorcery,
exuded a potent aroma of herbs and fire,
the air around her charged with the magic of her spells
and the fiery intensity of her betrayed heart.

Witch's Brew

Ingredients

2 oz Gin
1 oz Green Chartreuse
0.5 oz Lemon juice
Sprig of thyme for garnish

Recipe

Shake gin, Chartreuse, and lemon juice with ice.
Strain into a chilled glass and garnish with thyme.

Conjure the powerful magic and tragic betrayal of Medea in a cocktail that's as potent and fiery as her wrath.

Deep beneath the ocean's surface, Captain Nemo navigated the unknown in the Nautilus, surrounded by the briny depths of the sea, the air tinged with the mechanical scent of his submarine's interior, as mysterious as his own enigmatic persona.

Nautilus Depth

Ingredients

2 oz Navy Strength Gin
1 oz Blue Curacao
0.5 oz Lime juice
Pinch of sea salt

Recipe

Shake gin, Blue Curacao, lime juice, and sea salt with ice. Strain into a chilled glass.

Dive into the mysterious depths of Captain Nemo's world, where the salty essence of the sea meets the mechanical marvel of the Nautilus.

Along the murky Thames, Lizzie Hexam's world was imbued with the scent of river water and mud, a symbol of the mysteries and hidden depths of both the river and her own life in Dickens' London.

THAMES MYSTERY

Ingredients

2 oz London Dry Gin
1 oz Earl Grey tea syrup
0.5 oz Lemon juice
Lemon twist for garnish

Recipe

Brew Earl Grey tea, cool it, and make a syrup.
Shake gin, tea syrup, and lemon juice with ice.
Strain into a chilled glass and garnish with a lemon twist.

DRIFT THROUGH THE ENIGMATIC WATERS OF THE THAMES, WITH A COCKTAIL THAT CAPTURES THE MURKY MYSTERIES AND DEEP SECRETS OF LIZZIE HEXAM'S WORLD.

In the austere halls of Lowood School, Mr. Brocklehurst's stern presence was as rigid and unyielding as the scent of ink and polished wood, embodying the harsh discipline and moral rigidity of his educational regime.

Stern Discipline

Ingredients

2 oz Gin
1 oz Dry Vermouth
Dash of elderflower liqueur
Lemon twist for garnish

Recipe

Stir gin, vermouth, and elderflower liqueur with ice.
Strain into a chilled glass and garnish with a lemon twist.

Taste the strict, austere discipline of Mr. Brocklehurst, in a cocktail that's as rigid and uncompromising as his rule over Lowood School.

In the shadowed chambers of her castle, Lady Macbeth was enveloped in a scent as complex as her ambition, a haunting mix of floral perfume intertwined with the metallic edge of blood, a constant reminder of her part in the unfolding tragedy.

Guilty Rose

Ingredients

2 oz Gin
1 oz Rosewater
0.5 oz Cranberry juice
Splash of tonic water

Recipe

Shake gin, rosewater, and cranberry juice with ice.
Strain into a glass and top with tonic water.

Experience the chilling resolve of Lady Macbeth with a drink that blends delicate florals and a sharp, metallic edge.

In the oppressive heat of a St. Petersburg summer, Rodion Raskolnikov walked with the weight of guilt and philosophy, his mind as torrid as the hot stone and sweat of the city's air.

ST. PETERSBURG SUMMER

Ingredients

2 oz Vodka
1 oz Black tea syrup
0.5 oz Lemon juice
Sprig of mint

Recipe

Brew black tea and make a syrup.
Shake vodka, tea syrup, and lemon juice with ice.
Strain into a glass and garnish with mint.

Delve into the tormented soul of Raskolnikov with a cocktail that's as intense and brooding as a St. Petersburg summer.

The seductive Milady de Winter left a trail of allure and danger, her scent a captivating mix of seductive perfume with a whisper of poison, as deceptive and lethal as her charm.

Femme Fatale

Ingredients

2 oz Vodka
1 oz Chambord
0.5 oz Lime juice
Splash of cranberry juice

Recipe

Shake vodka, Chambord, lime juice, and cranberry juice with ice. Strain into a chilled glass.

UNCOVER THE SEDUCTIVE DANGER OF MILADY DE WINTER WITH A DRINK THAT'S AS INTOXICATING AND DEADLY AS HER SCHEMES.

In the eerie calm of the night, Carmilla drifted like a ghost, her presence haunting and ethereal, marked by the delicate fragrance of roses mixed with the cold, metallic scent of iron.

Vampire's Rose

Ingredients

2 oz Rose-infused Vodka
1 oz Crème de Cassis
0.5 oz Lemon juice
Edible rose petals for garnish

Recipe

Infuse vodka with rose petals.
Shake infused vodka, crème de cassis, and lemon juice with ice.
Strain into a glass and garnish with rose petals.

Embrace the haunting allure of Carmilla with a cocktail that blends the ethereal beauty of roses with a dark, vampiric twist

"Haunted by his own demons, Svidrigailov walked with the heavy air of guilt and moral corruption, the strong scent of vodka clinging to him, a reminder of his tormented soul."

Despair on the Rocks

Ingredients

2 oz Russian Vodka
1 oz Black currant liqueur
Dash of bitters
Lemon twist

Recipe

Stir vodka, liqueur, and bitters with ice.
Strain into a glass over ice and garnish with a lemon twist.

Contemplate the depths of despair and corruption with a cocktail as heavy and troubled as Svidrigailov's soul.

Frankenstein's monster, a being of unnatural creation, bore the chilling scents of laboratory chemicals and fresh earth, a walking reminder of the science that gave him life and the solitude that marked his existence.

MONSTROUS CREATION

Ingredients

2 oz Vodka
1 oz White crème de cacao
0.5 oz Lime juice
Dash of green food colouring

Recipe

Shake vodka, crème de cacao, lime juice, and food colouring with ice. Strain into a chilled glass.

EXPERIENCE THE CHILLING TALE OF CREATION GONE AWRY WITH A COCKTAIL AS STARK AND UNNERVING AS FRANKENSTEIN'S MONSTER.

The haunting presence of Sir Francis Varney, a mysterious vampire, lingered in the air like the musty scent of graveyards mixed with the unsettling trace of blood, as timeless and enigmatic as the night.

Transylvanian Nightshade

Ingredients

2 oz Black vodka
1 oz Chambord
0.5 oz Cranberry juice
Blackberry for garnish

Recipe

Shake vodka, Chambord, and cranberry juice with ice.
Strain into a chilled glass and garnish with a blackberry.

Embrace the shadowy world of a vampire with a drink that's as mysterious and haunting as Sir Francis Varney.

The Red Queen's domain was marked by a sharp command, her presence as striking as the scent of roses, combined with the metallic edge of authority, a reflection of her impulsive and domineering nature.

Off with Their Heads

Ingredients

2 oz Vodka
1 oz Rose syrup
0.5 oz Lemon juice
Splash of cranberry juice

Recipe

Shake vodka, rose syrup, lemon juice, and cranberry juice with ice. Strain into a chilled glass.

ASSERT YOUR COMMAND WITH A COCKTAIL
AS BOLD AND DEMANDING AS THE RED QUEEN HERSELF,
A BLEND OF ROSES' ALLURE AND THE SHARP BITE OF METAL.

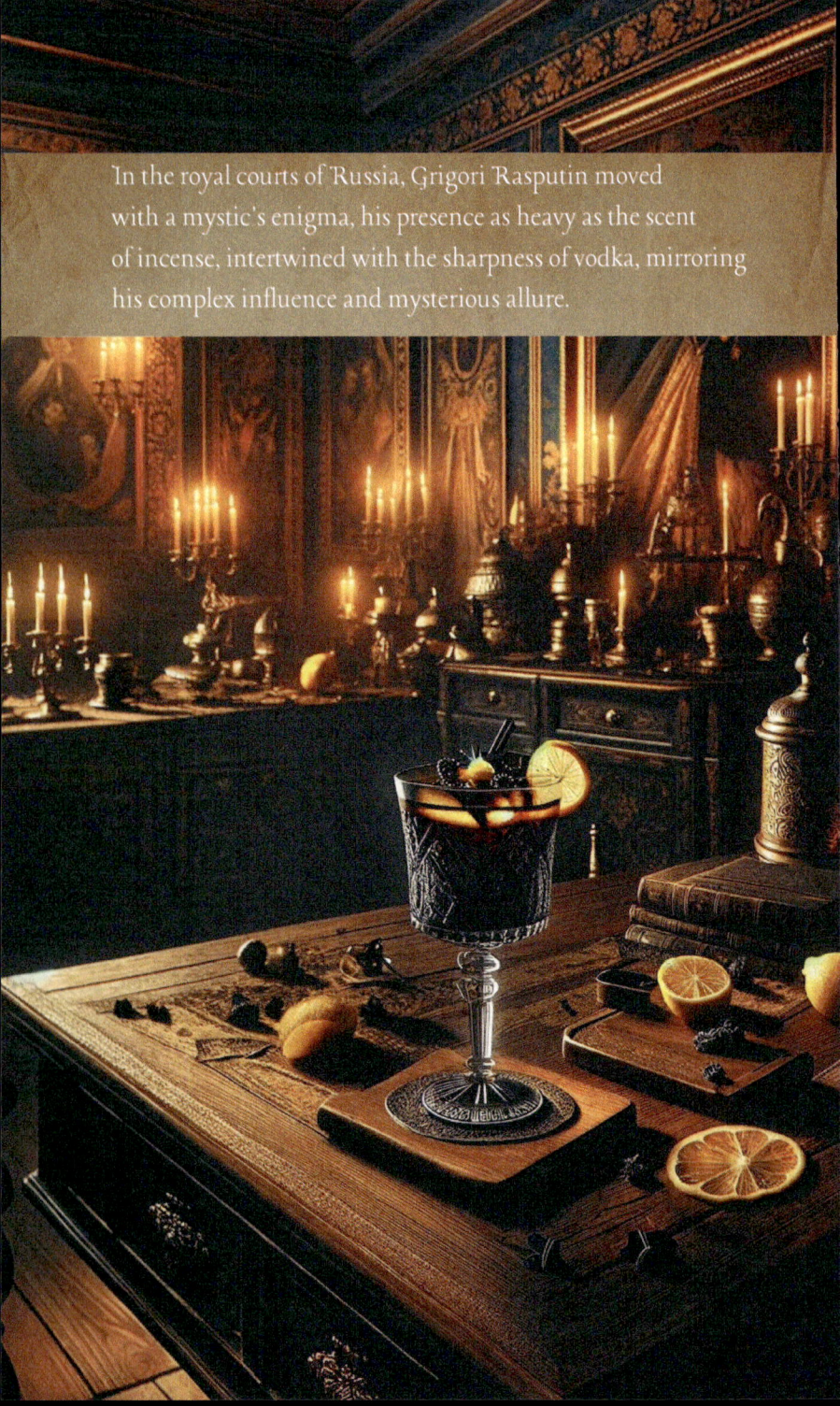

In the royal courts of Russia, Grigori Rasputin moved with a mystic's enigma, his presence as heavy as the scent of incense, intertwined with the sharpness of vodka, mirroring his complex influence and mysterious allure.

Mystic Elixir

Ingredients

2 oz Russian Vodka
1 oz Black tea syrup
0.5 oz Lemon juice
Dash of absinthe

Recipe

Brew black tea, cool it, and make a syrup.
Shake vodka, tea syrup, lemon juice, and absinthe with ice.
Strain into a chilled glass.

Delve into the mystic's enigma, where incense and vodka blend into a cocktail as complex and controversial as Rasputin's legacy.

Bourbon, whisky, whiskey

On the misty battlegrounds of Scotland, Macbeth's ambition hung heavily in the air, as cold and metallic as the blood-stained iron of his sword, a tangible reminder of his treacherous path to power.

SCOTTISH IRON

Ingredients

2 oz Scotch Whisky
0.5 oz Drambuie
Dash of Peychaud's bitters
Blood orange slice

Recipe

Stir whisky, Drambuie, and bitters with ice.
Strain into a glass and garnish with a blood orange slice.

Confront the raw ambition and haunting guilt of Macbeth with a drink as bold and complex as the Thane of Cawdor himself.

In the dark, foreboding chambers of Bluebeard's castle, the air was thick with the scent of old stone and blood, a lingering testament to the hidden horrors of his past wives' fate.

SECRET CHAMBER

Ingredients

2 oz Bourbon
1 oz Pomegranate juice
0.5 oz Simple syrup
Dash of Peychaud's bitters

Recipe

Shake bourbon, pomegranate juice, syrup, and bitters with ice. Strain into a glass over ice.

Unlock the dark secrets of Bluebeard with a cocktail that's as rich and foreboding as the hidden horrors in his castle.

On the windswept moors of Yorkshire,
Heathcliff was as untamed and passionate as the land itself,
the air around him filled with the scent of heather
and the stormy, brooding essence of his turbulent spirit.

Moorland Storm

Ingredients

2 oz Scotch Whisky
1 oz Drambuie
0.5 oz Lemon juice
Dash of Angostura bitters

Recipe

Shake whisky, Drambuie, lemon juice, and bitters with ice. Strain into a glass over ice.

Brave the passionate tempest of Heathcliff's love and revenge with a drink as wild and untamed as the moors themselves.

Abel Magwitch's rough life as a convict was marked by the damp, earthy smell of the marshes and the oppressive air of prison, reflecting his harsh existence and the unexpected twist of fate that connected him to Pip.

MARSHLAND ESCAPE

Ingredients

2 oz Bourbon
1 oz Sweet Vermouth
2 dashes Angostura bitters
Orange peel for garnish

Recipe

Stir bourbon, vermouth, and bitters with ice.
Strain into a chilled glass and garnish with orange peel.

NAVIGATE THE ROUGH TERRAIN
OF A CONVICT'S JOURNEY WITH A COCKTAIL
THAT BRINGS THE EARTHY, UNFORGIVING
ESSENCE OF THE MARSHLANDS TO YOUR GLASS.

On his Southern plantation, Simon Legree's presence
was as harsh and suffocating as the oppressive heat,
the air thick with the scent of cotton and the sweat
of his labourers, mirroring his brutal and tyrannical rule.

Plantation Fury

Ingredients

2 oz Rye Whiskey
1 oz Sweet tea
0.5 oz Lemon juice
Mint sprig for garnish

Recipe

Shake whiskey, sweet tea, and lemon juice with ice.
Strain into a glass and garnish with mint.

Feel the oppressive heat and brute force of a plantation with a drink that's as strong and relentless as Simon Legree's iron rule.

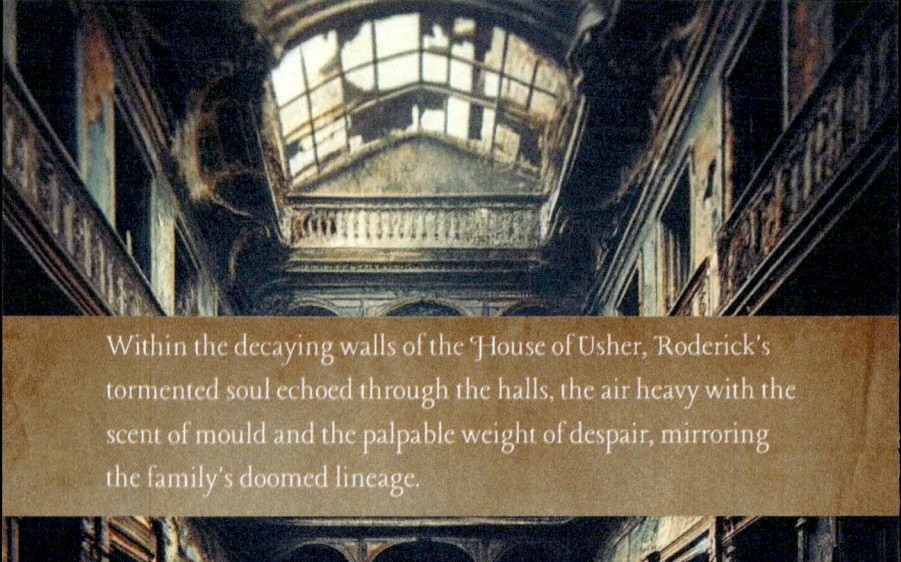

Within the decaying walls of the House of Usher, Roderick's tormented soul echoed through the halls, the air heavy with the scent of mould and the palpable weight of despair, mirroring the family's doomed lineage.

House of Usher

Ingredients

2 oz Scotch Whisky
1 oz Port wine
Dash of bitters
Orange peel for garnish

Recipe

Stir whisky, port wine, and bitters with ice.
Strain into a chilled glass and garnish with an orange peel.

Imbibe the melancholic essence of the Usher lineage, with a cocktail echoing the mould and despair of a family's tragic downfall.

In the whimsical realm of Wonderland,
the Queen of Hearts reigned with a capricious fury,
her presence a blend of sweet tarts and the fiery temper
of her whimsical tyranny.

WONDERLAND WRATH

Ingredients

2 oz Bourbon
1 oz Tart cherry juice
0.5 oz Simple syrup
Dash of bitters

Recipe

Shake bourbon, cherry juice, syrup, and bitters with ice.
Strain into a glass over ice.

FALL DOWN THE RABBIT HOLE OF WHIMSY AND RAGE, WHERE THE TARTNESS OF TARTS MEETS THE HEAT OF FURY IN A GLASS.

In the dimly lit corners of Fagin's den, the air was thick with the scent of old clothes and the clandestine dealings of London's underworld, as crafty and sly as the master thief himself.

Thief's Reward

Ingredients

2 oz Irish Whiskey
1 oz Apple cider
0.5 oz Honey syrup
Dash of cinnamon

Recipe

Shake whiskey, cider, honey syrup, and cinnamon with ice.
Strain into an ice-filled glass.

Step into the shadowy corners of Fagin's world, where the essence of old garments and ill-gotten gains is captured in a sly, robust cocktail.

In the gas-lit streets of Victorian London, Mr. Hyde moved with a duality as stark as the contrast between refined cologne and the sweat of unbridled savagery, an olfactory symbol of his fractured existence.

DUAL NATURE

Ingredients

2 oz Whisky
1 oz Coffee liqueur
0.5 oz Cream
Dash of Angostura bitters

Recipe

Shake whisky, coffee liqueur, and cream with ice.
Strain into a glass and add a dash of bitters.

EXPLORE THE DUALITY OF DR. JEKYLL AND MR. HYDE WITH A COCKTAIL THAT BALANCES SOPHISTICATED CHARM AND UNTAMED DARKNESS.

Wine, vermouth and sherry

In the shadowy corridors of his Transylvanian castle, Count Dracula's presence was as chilling as the musty scent of old books mixed with the ominous trace of blood, a timeless aroma of dread and allure.

Transylvanian Night

Ingredients

2 oz Red wine
1 oz Vodka
0.5 oz Chambord
Blackberry for garnish

Recipe

Shake wine, vodka, and Chambord with ice.
Strain into a chilled glass and garnish with a blackberry.

Succumb to the seductive darkness of Dracula with a drink as mysteriously alluring as the count himself.

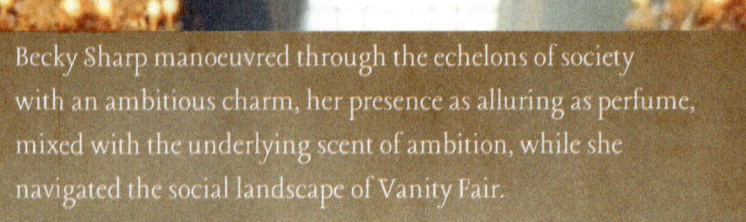

Becky Sharp manoeuvred through the echelons of society with an ambitious charm, her presence as alluring as perfume, mixed with the underlying scent of ambition, while she navigated the social landscape of Vanity Fair.

SOCIAL ASCENT

Ingredients

2 oz Prosecco
1 oz Aperol
0.5 oz Peach liqueur
Peach slice for garnish

Recipe

Pour Aperol and peach liqueur into a champagne flute.
Top with Prosecco and garnish with a peach slice.

Climb the social ladder with Becky Sharp, sipping on a cocktail that's as ambitious and cleverly crafted as her schemes in Vanity Fair.

The exotic and mysterious Dr. Fu Manchu exuded an air of Eastern intrigue, his presence marked by the heady aroma of opium and the subtle undertones of his complex, international schemes.

Eastern Enigma

Ingredients

2 oz Sake
1 oz Lychee liqueur
0.5 oz Lime juice
Lychee for garnish

Recipe

Shake sake, lychee liqueur, and lime juice with ice.
Strain into a chilled glass and garnish with a lychee.

Delve into the East-meets-West intrigue of Dr. Fu Manchu with a cocktail that balances exotic, mysterious flavors with a hint of hidden danger.

Rum

The infamous Long John Silver roamed the decks with the salty spirit of the sea clinging to him, his presence as bold and adventurous as the scent of gunpowder and rum that followed in his wake.

High Seas Adventure

Ingredients

2 oz Dark Rum
1 oz Pineapple juice
0.5 oz Lime juice
Pinch of sea salt

Recipe

Shake rum, pineapple juice, lime juice, and sea salt with ice. Strain into a glass filled with crushed ice.

Set sail on a swashbuckling adventure with a cocktail as bold and cunning as Long John Silver himself.

Edmond Đantès, transformed into the Count of Monte Cristo, moved with the richness and complexity of the sea and aged wine, his aura as deep and multifaceted as his quest for vengeance and redemption.

MONTE CRISTO'S REVENGE

Ingredients

2 oz Aged Rum
1 oz Port wine
0.5 oz Orange liqueur
Orange peel for garnish

Recipe

Stir rum, port wine, and orange liqueur with ice.
Strain into a chilled glass and garnish with an orange peel.

ESCAPE TO A TALE OF VENGEANCE AND TRANSFORMATION WITH A COCKTAIL AS LAYERED AND COMPLEX AS THE COUNT OF MONTE CRISTO.

Griffin, the Invisible Man, moved unseen, his presence marked only by the strange, elusive scent of laboratory chemicals, a testament to the bizarre experiment that erased him from sight.

INVISIBLE ELIXIR

Ingredients

2 oz Clear Rum
1 oz Coconut water
0.5 oz Lime juice
Splash of soda water

Recipe

Shake rum, coconut water, and lime juice with ice.
Strain into a glass and top with soda water.

Disappear into the mysterious world of Griffin with a cocktail that's as clear and enigmatic as the Invisible Man himself.

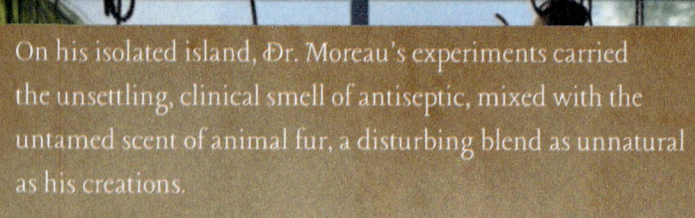

On his isolated island, Ðr. Moreau's experiments carried the unsettling, clinical smell of antiseptic, mixed with the untamed scent of animal fur, a disturbing blend as unnatural as his creations.

Island Experiment

Ingredients

2 oz White Rum
1 oz Pineapple juice
0.5 oz Cream of coconut
Dash of absinthe

Recipe

Shake rum, pineapple juice, and cream of coconut with ice.
Strain into a glass and add a dash of absinthe.

Venture into the realm of unnatural science with a drink that's as bizarre and unsettling as Dr. Moreau's creations

Frederick Bailey Deeming sailed the seas, his essence as vast and unfathomable as the ocean, the saltwater and ship wood scenting his journey with the brine of adventure and the shadow of his hidden horrors.

SAILOR'S DELIGHT

Ingredients

2 oz Dark Rum
1 oz Pineapple juice
0.5 oz Coconut cream
Dash of nutmeg

Recipe

Shake rum, pineapple juice, and coconut cream with ice. Strain into an ice-filled glass and sprinkle with nutmeg.

Set sail on a journey of mystery with a maritime cocktail as enigmatic as Deeming's own twisted travels.

In the cold, stone halls of his kingdom, Richard III's presence was as hard as the iron of his armour, the air around him charged with the ambition and turmoil of his reign, shadowed by the spectre of the Wars of the Roses.

Usurper's Draught

Ingredients

2 oz Dark Rum
1 oz Blackberry liqueur
0.5 oz Lemon juice
Dash of bitters

Recipe

Shake rum, blackberry liqueur, lemon juice, and bitters with ice. Strain into a glass with a large ice cube.

Taste the bitter ambition and twisted fate of a king with a drink as deep and complex as Richard III's tumultuous rule.

On the deck of the Jolly Roger, Captain Hook's menace filled the sea air, a blend of briny ocean and weathered leather, as fierce and relentless as his pursuit of Peter Pan in the world of Neverland.

Pirate's Demise

Ingredients

2 oz Dark Rum
1 oz Pomegranate juice
0.5 oz Lime juice
Dash of sea salt

Recipe

Shake rum, pomegranate juice, lime juice, and sea salt with ice. Strain into a glass filled with crushed ice.

Set sail with Captain Hook, feeling the tension of sea battles and pirate cunning, with a cocktail that's as bold and adventurous as Neverland's most feared villain.

Within the damp catacombs beneath his palazzo, Montresor enacted his revenge, the air filled with the earthy scent of wet stone and aged wine, as chilling as the cold finality of his actions.

Catacomb Elixir

Ingredients

2 oz Aged Rum
1 oz Sweet Vermouth
Dash of orange bitters
Orange twist

Recipe

Stir rum, vermouth, and bitters with ice.
Strain into a chilled glass and garnish with an orange twist.

Savour the dark, vengeful spirit of Montresor with a concoction as deep and mysterious as the catacombs in The Cask of Amontillado.

Aboard the Pequod, Captain Ahab's obsession filled the salty sea air, as briny and deep as the ocean he sailed, each wave carrying the scent of his singular pursuit of the white whale.

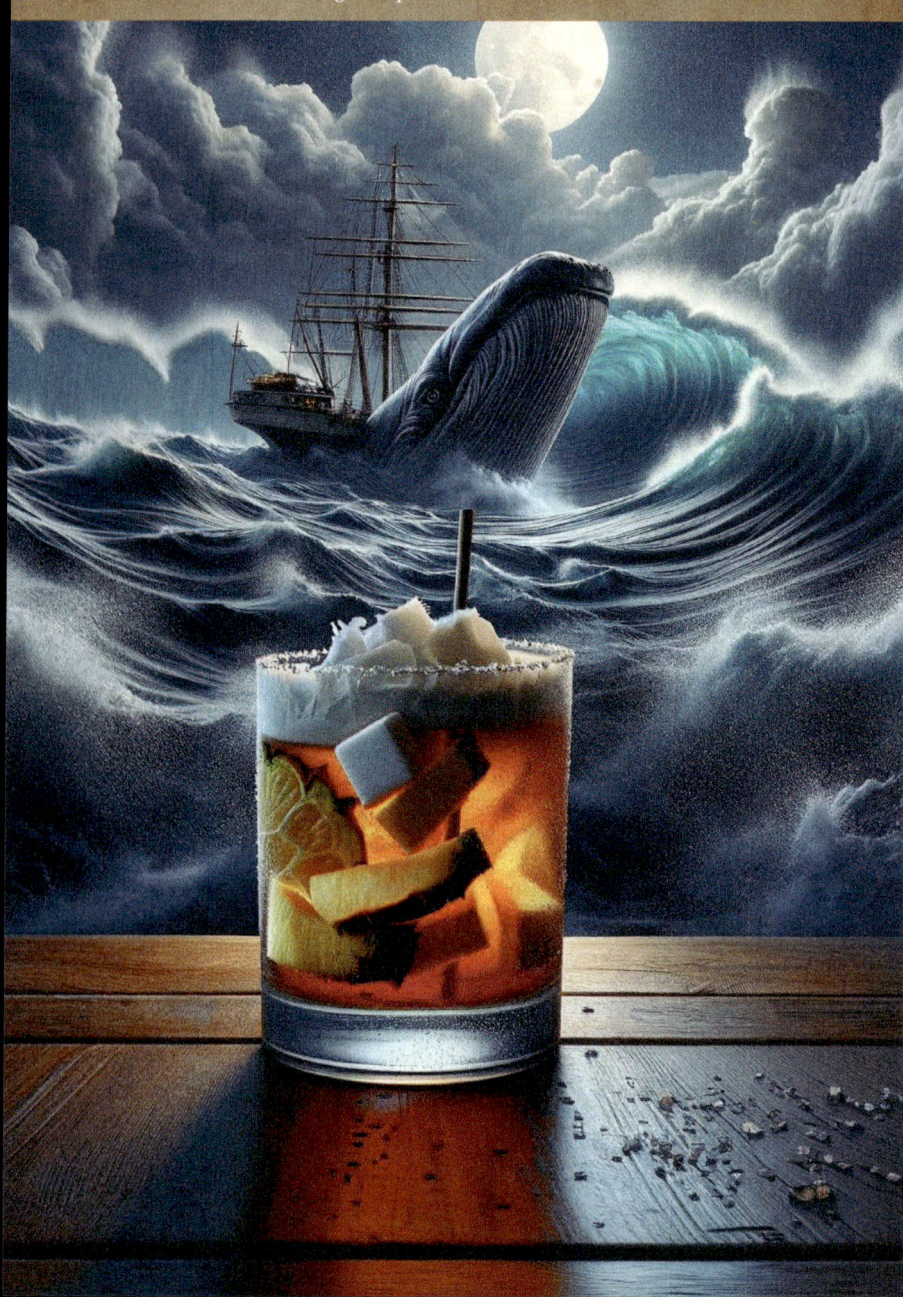

Ocean's Obsession

Ingredients

2 oz Dark Rum
1 oz Pineapple juice
0.5 oz Coconut cream
Dash of sea salt

Recipe

Shake rum, pineapple juice, coconut cream, and sea salt with ice. Strain into a glass filled with crushed ice.

Embark on a relentless pursuit with Ahab's obsession, captured in a cocktail as briny and bold as the open sea.

Tequila and Liqueur

Amidst the intrigue of Venice, Iago weaved his plots with a scent as acrid as bitter almonds, his manipulations leaving a trail of deceit and betrayal that lingered long after his machinations.

Venetian Deceit

Ingredients

2 oz Amaretto
1 oz Bourbon
0.5 oz Lemon juice
Almond for garnish

Recipe

Shake amaretto, bourbon, and lemon juice with ice.
Strain into a chilled glass and garnish with an almond.

Unravel the cunning deceit of Iago with a cocktail that's as subtly bitter and twisted as Shakespeare's notorious villain.

Clytemnestra moved through the halls of Mycenae with a regal air, her presence as intoxicating as incense and as sharp as steel, echoing her vengeful plot within the walls of her ancient kingdom.

Royal Revenge

Ingredients

2 oz Ouzo
1 oz Pomegranate juice
0.5 oz Lemon juice
Splash of club soda

Recipe

Shake ouzo, pomegranate juice, and lemon juice with ice.
Strain into a glass and top with club soda.

Revel in the intoxicating mix of power and vengeance with a drink that captures Clytemnestra's fierce and regal essence.

Brandy and Cognac

In the midst of revoluntionary fervour, Madame Ðefarge sat quietly knitting, the wool in her hands carrying the scent of gunpowder, as potent and vengeful as her plans for those entangled in her web.

REVOLUTIONARY SPIRIT

Ingredients

2 oz Cognac
1 oz Black tea syrup
0.5 oz Lemon juice
Dash of gunpowder tea (for aroma)

Recipe

Brew black tea and make a syrup.
Shake Cognac, tea syrup, and lemon juice with ice.
Strain into a glass and garnish with a pinch of gunpowder tea.

KNIT TOGETHER INTRIGUE AND REBELLION WITH A DRINK THAT CAPTURES MADAME DEFARGE'S FIERY SPIRIT AND REVOLUTIONARY FERVOUR.

Alec d'Urberville carried the charm of the Victorian countryside, his presence tinged with the rich scent of brandy and the earthy smell of hay, masking the underlying deception of his character.

Victorian Seduction

Ingredients

2 oz Brandy
1 oz Apple cider
0.5 oz Honey syrup
Dash of cinnamon

Recipe

Shake brandy, cider, honey syrup, and cinnamon with ice.
Strain into a chilled glass.

Indulge in the deceptive charm of Alec d'Urberville with a cocktail that's as smooth and alluring as his wiles.

Vautrin, lurking in the shadows of Balzac's Paris, carried with him the scent of tobacco and the grimy essence of the city's streets, as complex and dangerous as his manipulative schemes.

Parisian Underworld

Ingredients

2 oz Cognac
1 oz Red wine
0.5 oz Simple syrup
Dash of orange bitters

Recipe

Stir cognac, wine, syrup, and bitters with ice.
Strain into a chilled glass.

Navigate the treacherous underbelly of Paris with a cocktail as dark and cunning as Vautrin's schemes.

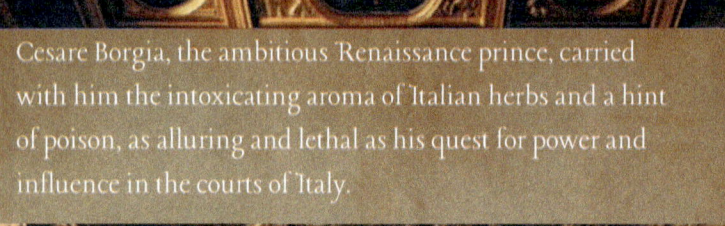

Cesare Borgia, the ambitious Renaissance prince, carried with him the intoxicating aroma of Italian herbs and a hint of poison, as alluring and lethal as his quest for power and influence in the courts of Italy.

Renaissance Ambition

Ingredients

2 oz Grappa
1 oz Sweet vermouth
0.5 oz Amaretto
Orange twist for garnish

Recipe

Stir grappa, vermouth, and amaretto with ice.
Strain into a glass and garnish with an orange twist.

Taste the ruthless ambition of Cesare Borgia in a cocktail that's as bold and captivating as the prince's own quest for power.

"High in the bell tower of Notre Dame, Quasimodo existed in solitude, the air filled with the scent of old stone and aged wood, echoing the loneliness and timeless beauty of his sanctuary.

Bell Tower Solitude

Ingredients

2 oz Calvados
1 oz Dry Vermouth
0.5 oz Benedictine
Apple slice for garnish

Recipe

Stir Calvados, vermouth, and Benedictine with ice.
Strain into a chilled glass and garnish with an apple slice.

Ring in the poignant solitude of Notre Dame with a drink that echoes the quiet beauty and age-old stories of Quasimodo's bell tower retreat.

In the grand halls of Elsinore, Claudius moved with the heavy aroma of rich wine and hidden poison, a deceptive blend that mirrored the corrupt heart beneath his kingly facade.

Regal Poison

Ingredients

2 oz Aged Brandy
0.5 oz Port wine
0.5 oz Amaretto
1 dash of Bitters
A small drop of Absinthe
Gold leaf or edible gold dust for garnish

Recipe

In a mixing glass, combine the brandy, port wine, and amaretto.
Add a dash of bitters.
Add a small drop of absinthe – just enough to give the drink a slight edge without overpowering the other flavours.
Fill the mixing glass with ice and stir gently until it's well-chilled.
Strain the cocktail into a chilled coupe glass
Garnish with a piece of gold leaf or a sprinkle of edible gold dust.

Taste the dark allure of power and guilt that defines Claudius, in a cocktail as rich and intoxicating as his ill-gotten throne.

In the hidden catacombs beneath the Paris Opera House, the Phantom's presence lingered like a haunting melody, the air infused with the scent of old music sheets and the warmth of candle wax, as enigmatic as his masked persona.

Opera's Shadow

Ingredients

2 oz Cognac
1 oz Amaretto
0.5 oz Cream
Dash of vanilla extract

Recipe

Shake cognac, amaretto, cream, and vanilla with ice.
Strain into a chilled glass.

Embrace the haunting melody of the Paris Opera with a drink that captures the Phantom's melancholic essence, blending the romance of music with the mystery of shadows.

Rodolphe Boulanger moved through the French countryside with a seducer's ease, his presence tinged with the rustic scents of hay and tobacco, a deceptive charm masking his fleeting romances.

TEMPTER'S TOAST

Ingredients

2 oz Cognac
1 oz Sweet Vermouth
0.5 oz Amaretto
Tobacco leaf for garnish (optional)

Recipe

Stir cognac, vermouth, and amaretto with ice.
Strain into a glass and garnish with a tobacco leaf if available.

INDULGE IN THE FLEETING PLEASURES OF RODOLPHE'S SEDUCTION, WHERE THE RUSTIC AROMA OF HAY MEETS THE SMOOTH ALLURE OF TOBACCO IN A BEGUILING DRINK.

Javert's pursuit through the streets of Paris was unyielding, his presence as rigid and steadfast as the scent of gunpowder, mixed with the essence of the city's cobblestone streets, a symbol of his relentless quest for justice.

UNRELENTING JUSTICE

Ingredients

2 oz Armagnac
1 oz Sweet Vermouth
0.5 oz Cognac-based orange liqueur
Orange peel for garnish

Recipe

Stir Armagnac, vermouth, and orange liqueur with ice.
Strain into a chilled glass and garnish with orange peel.

Chase the unyielding scent of justice with a cocktail that mirrors Javert's steadfast pursuit, combining the smoky intensity of gunpowder with the rich, complex layers of Parisian streets.

Other

The cunning Count Fosco moved through the Victorian society with a scent as sophisticated as fine cologne, mixed with the subtle undertone of ink, a reflection of his manipulative intelligence and dark secrets.

Sinister Sophistication

Ingredients

2 oz Aperol
1 oz Gin
0.5 oz Lemon juice
Splash of prosecco

Recipe

Shake Aperol, gin, and lemon juice with ice.
Strain into a glass and top with prosecco.

Delve into the manipulative mind of Count Fosco with a drink that's as refined and sinister as the count himself.

The Controversial Cocktail Club

continues in Volume 1

Your cocktail notes

Your cocktail notes

Your cocktail notes

Your cocktail notes

Printed in Great Britain
by Amazon